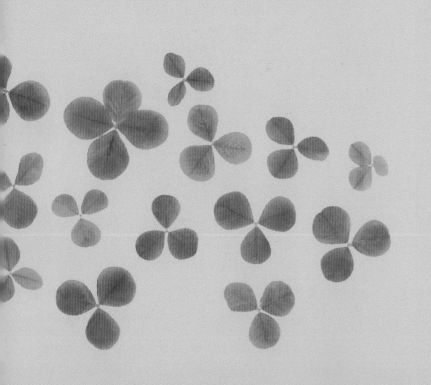

Seasons

playBac
PUBLISHING
More.Brain.Power

Spring, Summer,
Fall, and Winter:
There is a reason for every season!

The changing seasons reflect the dynamic beauty of the world around us. Eye Like Seasons is the perfect introduction to the clues that nature gives us, indicating that change is on the way, Summer is in the air, Fall is in the wind, Winter is near, and Spring can't be far behind!

What are you waiting for? Begin your journey through the seasons of the year. Turn the page and let's go!

Key to season icons:

Spring

Summer

Fall

Winter

Spring has sprung !

In the spring everything grows.
Buds are about to become flowers, but do they know?
Babies are born, both animals and plants.
Spring's in the air! Time for a song and a dance!

bird's nest

buds

4

seedling

rabbit family

dew on grass

dew on a flower

6

It's wet out there !

Who knew?
Tiny drops of water are called dew!
But fog is just clouds near to the ground.
It's low and it's wet and it doesn't make a sound.

fog

dew on a ladybug

cornfield

First to sprout !

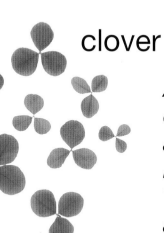

clover

*Asparagus points are
called "spears,"
and when the corn is grown,
it will have "ears."
The first plants of the season
are the pioneers.
The greenest green,
spring's souvenirs!*

green wheat

asparagus

9

The beauty

daffodil

hyacinth

of blooms

cherry blossoms

The colors of spring are truly awesome!
Yellow, blue, and pink, each pretty blossom!
The air is filled with sweet perfume.
It's amazing to see spring bloom.

Tadpole to frog

tadpole

tadpole

tadpoles

When the tadpole loses his tail,
the adult frog is unveiled.
Once a great swimmer,
he now has land to conquer.
The frog is happy to become
a great hopper!

young frog

adult frog

13

toad

snail

It's raining, it's pouring!

It sure is wet,
and we're all set!
For springtime showers, all kinds of flowers,
and a bright rainbow.
The rain helps everything to grow!

rainbow

chrysalis

caterpillar

It may look strange
and what a way to rearrange!
The caterpillar makes a huge exchange:
He now has wings instead of toes.
Look up and away: There he goes!

Caterpillar

butterflies

nto butterfly !

Signs of the season

salamander

ladybugs

water lily

It's finally warm and now it is summer.
The dragonfly beats his wings – he is the drummer!
Everyone begins to emerge,
over on the lily pads, the ladybugs will converge.
The salamander has just started to stir.
These signs of the season are what he prefers.

dragonfly

Seed into plant

The little seed will soon be a bean.
And from start to finish, it stays bright, bright green.
Ready, set, go!
The seed will grow and grow.
The little seedling
puts on quite a fashion show!

seed

seedling

bean plant

bean

Color burst !

The sunflowers are happy
    to be yellow.
They ask the bee,
"What about you, little fellow?"
"I'm just trying to blend in!
I've got some pollen on my shin!
And I think the corn is looking
for a scarecrow."

corn

eld of sunflowers

bee and pollen

It's hot out there

sun

footprints

sand

seashell

The bright sun shines
on the sea.
And over there,
a leaning palm tree.
Beneath it, a pattern
crosses the sand.
The palm frond shadow,
neatly fanned.

palm tree

shadow

These are the longest days.
The earth is warmed by the sun's rays.
Tomatoes ripen and we take holidays,
enjoy watermelon and big, bright bouquets.

tomatoes

Summer peaks!

watermelon

stormy sky

wheat field

27

Summer into fall

green
maple
leaf

beech tree in summer

*Why does summer seem so brief?
It's a good question to ask a leaf.
With the cooler weather, leaves
change their color altogether.
Green turns to brown and soon
all the leaves have fallen down.*

beech tree in fall

brown maple leaf

Fall is golden

The baled hay is in the field.
The beauty of fall is revealed!
The last flowers of the season
bloom and unfold,
showing the deep golden-orange
of the marigold.
The apples are ripe and ready to pic
gold and red and the color of brick.

marigolds

apples

hay bales in field

Signs of the season

pumpkin

grapes

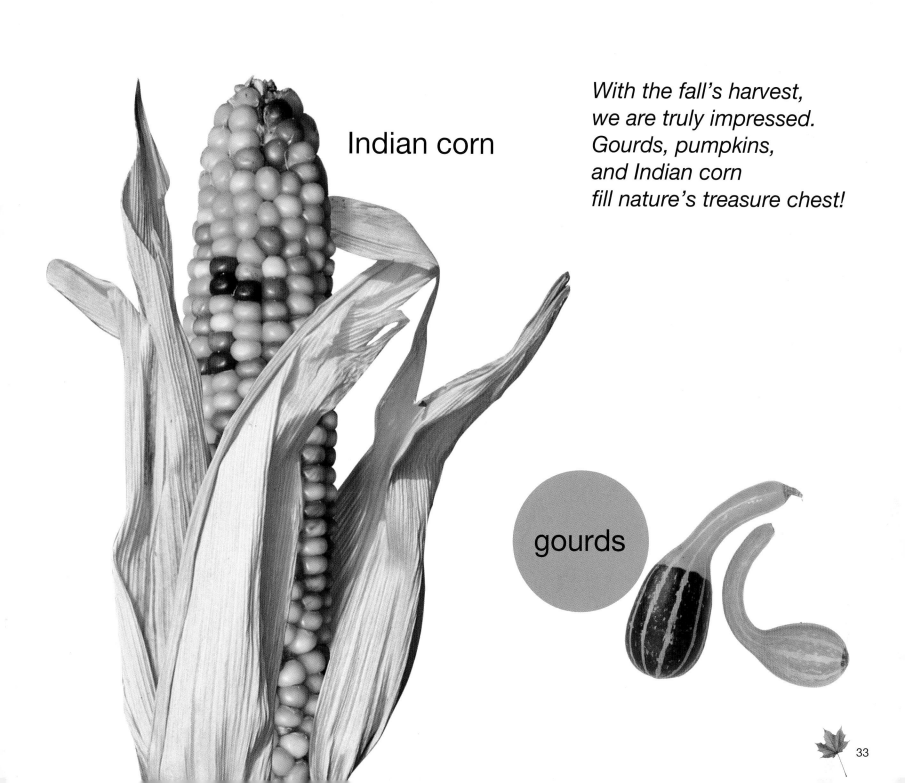

Indian corn

With the fall's harvest,
we are truly impressed.
Gourds, pumpkins,
and Indian corn
fill nature's treasure chest!

gourds

Fall colors

*The fox is happy to jump
in the leaves.
In and out of them he weaves.
Red, orange, and yellow make
him feel very mellow.
He's quite content, he believes.*

red fox

autumn
leaves

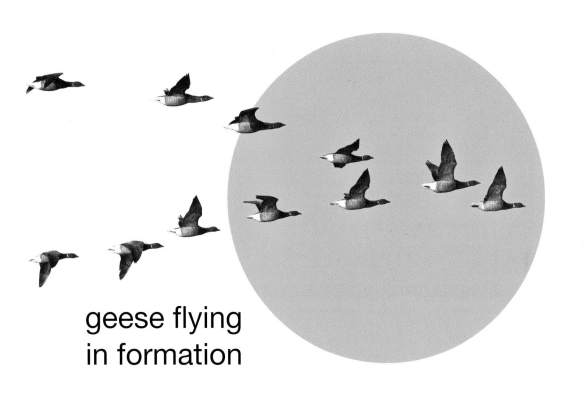

geese flying
in formation

Preparing for winter,
the birds head south.
The squirrel does not want
to live hand-to-mouth.
He won't need to roam,
he gathers nuts to fill his home.
To him, fall is a beautiful poem.

mushrooms

Fall back

geese

acorns

squirrel

hazelnuts

Hold on to your hat

You may not see anything,
but it certainly is real.
And as these photographs reveal,
you'll need to be quite disciplined
to withstand the full force
of a strong fall wind.

snowy egret

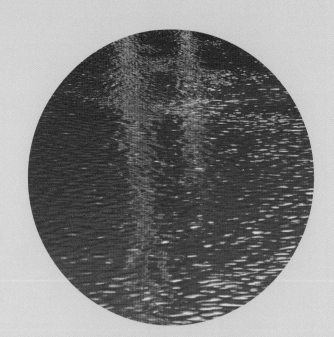

wind on water

grass field

horse

Fall into

falling leaves

The autumn leaves begin to fall,
until there are none left at all.
By winter the beech tree is bare,
she has nothing at all left to wear.
When her leaves begin to stir,
there is no way to prepare!

winter

beech tree in winter

When the world is covered in frost
everything looks quite glossed.
Icy crystals blanket the berries.
But this is all necessary:
As fall moves into winter,
everything seems temporary.

frost on leaves

42

frost on berries

A chill in the air

Time for winter coats!

brown bear

The brown bear stays warm
all winter long.
"My thick fur coat keeps me strong!"
Getting ready to hibernate,
the animals get along.
Once their fur is thick enough,
they'll all say, "So long!"
The skunk isn't worried;
she doesn't have a care.
It's not her coat, but her smell,
that makes us beware!

wolf

skunk

holly

evergreen tree

Signs of

Here you see the green-and-red holly.
The cedar waxwing looks quite jolly.
What a pretty winter scene:
The pinecone and the evergreen.

cedar waxwing

pinecone

he season

snowflake

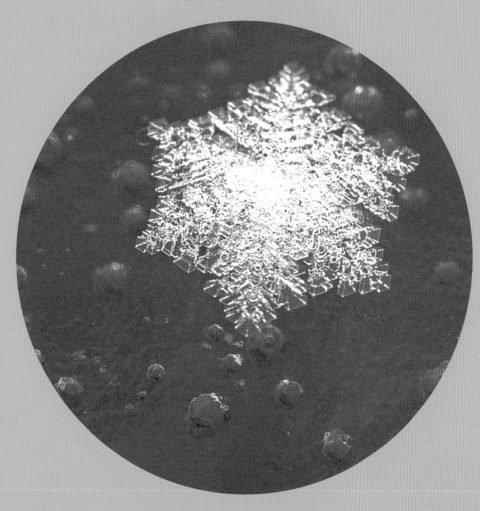

It's cold out there!

icicles

frozen lake

Frozen water makes
icicles and snowflakes.
Be careful! Make no mistake:
Watch your step on the frozen lake.
It's cold out there, for goodness' sake!

A good time to hide

arctic fox

In the frozen snow,
these animals don't always show.
They're very careful to stay out of sight,
trying hard not to get frostbite.
But when they do come out to play,
they are delighted with the whiteness
of the day.

snowy owl

arctic hare

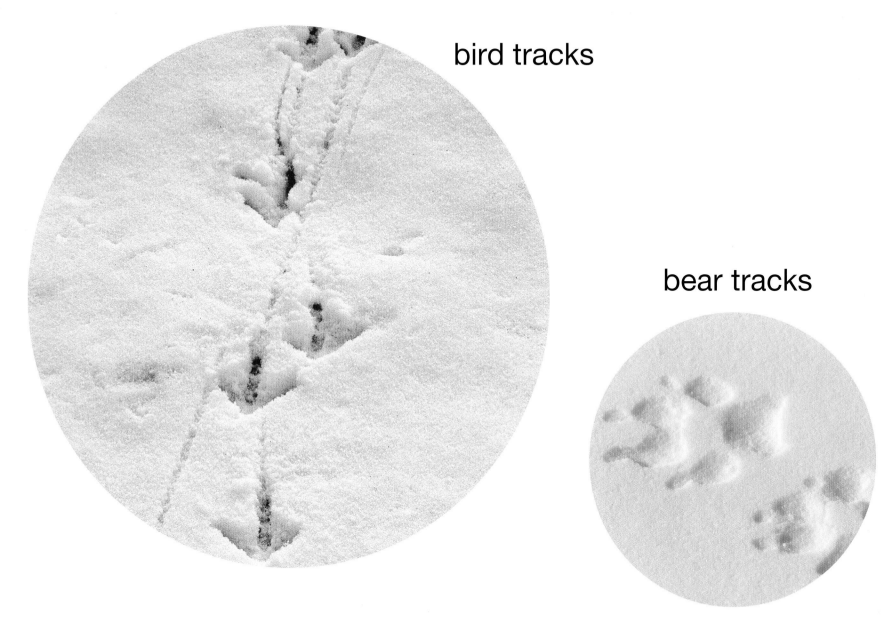

bird tracks

bear tracks

Who goes there?

crows

The snow offers clues,
whether claws, paws, or shoes,
to who is out of the zoos and who has
broken their curfews.
We can see who's been out in the snow,
and who's been running on tiptoes.

snow

snowdrops

The year begins anew

spring melt

crocus

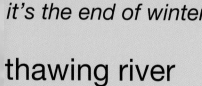

Winter is about to say, "Good-bye."
And spring's first flowers will try and try
to peek out of the snow and drip-dry.
The yellow crocuses are about to bloom,
pushing up to see if there is room.
The warming temperatures make them assume,
it's the end of winter's cold and gloom!

thawing river

Acknowledgments:

Play Bac Publishing wishes to thank all the teachers, mothers, and children who have helped develop the **eye like** series.

SPECIAL THANKS to: Alain Pichlak & Frédéric Michaud (ikopank), Christopher Hardin, Cheryl Weisman, Anne Burrus, Paula Manzanero and Emmanuel Roc.

Copyright © 2009
by Play Bac Publishing
USA, Inc.

ISBN-13: 978-1-60214-083-7

Play Bac Publishing USA, Inc.
225 Varick Street, New York, NY 10014-4381

infospbusa@playbac.fr
Contact number : +12126147725

Printed in Singapore by TWP

Distributed by
Black Dog & Leventhal Publishers, Inc.
151 West 19th Street, New York, NY 10011

April/2009

Photography credits:

Meaning of the letters:
h : top ; b : bottom ; d : right ; g : left ; c : center.

BIOSPHOTO: Cordier Sylvain 50g ; Dauriac Roger 14-15c ; Douillet Joël 21d ; Hette Stéphane 22 ; Klein J.-L. & Hube 45d, 51d ; Maurer André 48g ; Muller Fred 18-19c ; NouN 34-35 ; Perelle Christophe 50-51c ; Renard Franck 37g ; Robert Henno / Wildlife Pictures 53c ; Sidamon-Pesson Christophe 53 ; Thiriet Claudius 9d, 18hd, 18c, 19hg, 31.

CORBIS: © Corbis 2, 8, 20-21 ; Arthur Morris 38d ; Aso Fujita 55g ; Craig Tuttle 42g, 54 ; Eric Cahan 41 ; Frank Krahmer 5g ; Frank Lukasseck 29g ; Frithjof Hirdes 40c ; Gary Carter 7g ; Gerolf Kalt 28g ; Gerry Whitmont 46g ; Maximilian Stock Ltd 26g ; Micha Pawlitzki 39.

EYEDEA: Bourseiller Philippe / Hoa-Qui 3h, 48-49 ; Claye Monique / Jacana 54d ; Cordier Sylvain / Jacana 16d ; John Cancalosi / NPL / Jacana 4d ; Krasemann Stephen J. / Jacana 44 ; Mark Hamblin / Imagestate 6d ; Redares Bruno 27 ; SGM 37bg ; Silvester Hans / Rapho 39d ; Steve Satushek 14.

GETTY: Allison Dinner 33bd ; Art Wolfe 6g ; Christina Bollen / GAP Photos 23d ; Cyndy Black / Robert Harding World Imagery 7d ; Dave King 10g ; DKAR Images / Stone 25g ; Don Farrall / Photodisc back cover, 36b ; Dorling Kindersley front cover, 1, 19, 30-31c, 37hd ; Ellen Rooney 49d ; Gail Shumway 17d ; Gary Yeowell 15d ; Geoff Brightling / Dorling Kindersley 3d, 13d, 18g, 47g ; Geoff Dann 12c ; Grant Faint 24 ; Guy Edwardes 1h, 47d ; Hiller, Jost 9bg ; Jean-Michel Georges 32d ; Jim Franco 25d ; Julie Pigula / GAP Photos 10-11c ; Kai Stiepel 32g ; Kathy Collins back cover, 40-41 ; Kim Taylor 16g ; Kim Taylor and Jane Burton 12g, 12d, 12-13c ; Mark Bolton / GAP Photos 30g ; Peter Miller 55d ; Rich Iwasaki / Stone spine, front cover ; Rosemary Calvert 8-9c ; Ross M. Horowitz 11d ; Steve Gorton 23g, 37bd ; Steve Shott 5d ; T.Kitchen and V. Hurst 17g ; Tohoku Color Agency 38g.

PHOTONONSTOP: Leslie West 46d ; S. Barçon 26d.

SUNSET: Brake 52d ; Cattlin Nigel 52g ; Huguet P. - Dubief M. 42-43c ; imagebroker.net spine, front cover ; Janes Ernie 53hd ; Juniors Bild Archiv 45bg ; Philipps Michel 43 ; Smith Gary K. 36h.

OTHER PHOTOS: DR.

In the same series: